D0833717

Life is hard
        and then you nap.

Rachael Hale is an award-winning,
internationally recognised photographer
who specializes in animal portraiture.

Her creative flamboyance with her subjects
has created a new genre in animal photography
and her images have been published
on greetings cards, calendars, posters,
stationery and books worldwide.

Rachael lives in Auckland, New Zealand,
with her three cats Edmund, Gianni and Versace.

LIFE IS HARD AND THEN YOU NAP
© 2005 Rachael Hale Photography Ltd.
All rights reserved. Rachael Hale is a registered trademark of
Rachael Hale Photography Limited.
www.rachaelhale.com

Edited by J. Rose Barber
Photography courtesy of RACHAEL HALE PHOTOGRAPHY LTD.
Design by WPL

Printed in China
Published by WPL 2005

ISBN 1-904264-42-5

WPL
The Perfume Factory
140 Wales Farm Road
London W3 6UG
Tel: +44 (0) 208 993 7268
Fax: +44 (0) 208 993 8041
email: info@wpl.eu.com
www.wpl.eu.com

There can't be a better life than a cat's -
doing what they like, when they like,
as much as they like.

[RICARDO PHILIPS]

It's hard not to envy a cat -

they know how to **relax**

without having a care in the world.

[ANON]

A cat can **sleep** anywhere at any time.

There is no such thing as a cat with insomnia.

[JACQUELINE FRANCIS]

Cats allow us to love them,

for which we should be duly grateful.

[ANNE BROWN]

When a cat **adopts** you

there is nothing to be done about it

except to put up with it until the wind changes.

[T. S. ELIOT]

Everyone knows

there's no such thing

as a cat owner.

[NICHOLAS HAWORTH]

Cats know how to obtain food without labour,

shelter without confinement,

and love without penalties.

[ADRIAN GEORGE]

A cat can **purr** it's way out of anything.

[RUTH HANLON]

Cats seem to go on the principle

that it never does any harm to

ask for what you want.

Dogs believe they are human.

Cats **believe** they are God.

[ANON]

Cats were put into the world

to disprove the dogma that

all things were created to serve man.

[PAUL GRAY]

Cats come when they're called,

unless they have something more

interesting to do.

[ANON]

Women and cats will do as they please,

and men and dogs should relax

and get used to the idea.

[ROBERT A. HEINLEIN]

Cats don't like change

without their permission.

[ROGER CARAS]

Dogs have owners, cats have staff.

[ANON]

Many years ago,

cats were **worshipped** as gods.

Cats have never forgotten this.

[ANON]

Cats are connoiseurs of comfort.

[JAMES HERRIOT]

If there is one spot of sun
spilling onto the floor,
a cat will find it and soak it up.

No amount of time

    can erase the memory of a good cat,

    and no amount of masking tape can ever

totally remove his fur from your couch.

[ANON]

Prowling his own quiet backyard
or asleep by the fire,
he is still only a whisker
away from the wilds.

[JEAN BURDEN]

To err is human, to purr is feline.

[AUTHOR UNKNOWN]

In a cat's world,

all things belong to **cats**.

[ENGLISH PROVERB]

Cats don't come when they're called,

they take a message and get back to you later.

[WILFRED P. LAMPTON]

As we all know,

cats now rule the world.

[ANON]

Cats are absolute individuals, with their own ideas about everything, including the people they own.

[JOHN DINGMAN]

A dog is a man's best friend.

A cat is a cat's best friend.

[ANON]

If there were to be a universal sound depicting peace,

I would surely vote for the purr.

[AUTHOR UNKNOWN]

A cat's a **cat**

and that's that.

[AMERICAN FOLK SAYING]